YOUR BOOK OF SOCCER

The YOUR BOOK Series

Acting
Aeromodelling
Animal Drawing
Aquaria
Astronomy
Badminton
Ballet
Bridges
Butterflies and Moths
The Way a Car Works
Cake Making and
    Decorating
Camping
Card Games
Card Tricks
Chemistry
Chess
Coin Collecting
Computers
Confirmation
Contract Bridge
Cricket
Medieval and Tudor
    Costume
17th & 18th Century
    Costume
19th Century Costume
Dinghy Sailing
The Earth
Electronics
Embroidery
Engines and Turbines
The English Bible
Fencing
Figure Drawing
Film-Making

Fishes
Flower Arranging
Flower Making
Flying
Freshwater Life
Furniture
Golf
Gymnastics
Hovercraft
The Human Body
Judo
Kites
Knitted Toys
Knitting and Crochet
Knots
Landscape Drawing
Light
Magic
Maps and Map
    Reading
Mental Magic
Model Car Racing
Modelling
Money
Music
Paper Folding
Parliament
Patchwork
Party Games
Patience
Pet Keeping
Photographing Wild
    Life
Photography
Keeping Ponies
Prehistoric Britain

Puppetry
The Recorder
Roman Britain
Rugger
Sea Angling
The Seashore
Self-Defence
Sewing
Shell Collecting
Skating
Soccer
Sound
Space Travel
Squash
Stamps
Surnames
Survival Swimming
    and Life Saving
Swimming
Swimming Games and
    Activities
Table Tennis
Table Tricks
Tape Recording
Television
Tennis
Trampolining
Trees
Underwater Swimming
Veteran and
    Edwardian Cars
Vintage Cars
Watching Wild Life
Waterways
The Weather
Woodwork

Your Book of
SOCCER

by

Robin Trimby

Illustrated by

Doriel Trimby, A.R.C.A.

FABER AND FABER
3 Queen Square
London

First published in 1968
by Faber and Faber Limited
3 Queen Square London WC1
Second edition 1971
Reprinted 1975
Printed in Great Britain by
Latimer Trend & Company Ltd Plymouth

ISBN 0 571 04752 1

Acknowledgements

THE AUTHOR wishes to acknowledge the assistance of the young footballers of Shrewsbury School who have enthusiastically helped to illustrate this book. He also wishes to thank Elizabeth Jones for translating his handwriting into legible type; John Dent for his excellent services as photographer; Doriel Trimby for her sketches and diagrams; and the Press Association for permission to use their photographs for Plates 22, 26, 35, 38 and 39.

Contents

Introduction   *page* 15

1. PREPARING FOR THE GAME   19
   How to Train   19
   What to Wear   21

2. IMPROVING YOUR SKILL   24
   Kicking   24
   Trapping   31
   Heading   35
   Tackling   39
   Dribbling   42
   Screening   42
   Throw-In   43
   Individual Practices   45

3. POSITIONAL PLAY   49
   Goalkeeper   49
   Full-Backs   54
   Centre-Half   58
   Wing-Halves   60
   Wing-Forwards   62

Inside-Forwards *page* 64

Centre-Forward 68

4. Understanding the Game 72

5. Learning from the Professionals 79

6. Lessons from the 1970 World Cup 87

Illustrations

PLATES

1, 2.   Working hard in training   *page* 20

3, 4, 5.   The low instep pass   26

6, 7, 8.   The lofted pass   28

9.   Kicking with the inside of the foot   29

10.   Kicking with the outside of the foot   30

11.   The volley   31

12.   Trapping—with the inside of the foot   32

13.   Trapping—with the outside of the foot   32

14.   Trapping—on the volley   33

15.   The chest trap—concave   34

16.   The chest trap—convex   34

17.   The thigh trap   35

18.   Heading—the simple pass   36

19.   Jumping and heading   37

20.   The defensive header   37

21, 22.   The header at goal   38

23, 24.   The block tackle   39

25. The sliding tackle   *page* 41
26. The professional tackle   41
27. Screening   43
28. The throw-in   44
29. Practise on your own   47
30, 31, 32. Goalkeeper—three ways of catching
        the ball   50
33. Goalkeeper—the two-fisted punch   51
34, 35. Goalkeeper—diving at a forward's feet   53
36. 'Laying-off' a pass   70
37. Positioning at a corner kick   81
38. The bicycle kick   84
39. Poise and balance   86
40. The decisive goal   91
41. Brazilian Magic   93
42. All that's best in football   95

FIGURES IN TEXT

1. How to tie your boots   22
2. Kicking with the instep   26
3. Kicking with the inside of the foot   29
4. Kicking with the outside of the foot   30
5. Practise heading on your own   46
6, 7. Goalkeeper narrowing the angle   52
8. Positional play of a full-back   55
9. Positional play of a full-back   56
10. Defender 'containing' an attacker   57

11.	Defender 'containing' an attacker	*page* 58
12.	Overlapping	59
13.	The double centre-half	62
14.	Positional play of a winger	63
15.	Wingers—the centre	65
16.	Passes of the inside-forward	66
17.	Positional play of the inside-forward	67
18.	Positional play of the centre-forward	69
19.	Positional play of the centre-forward	70
20.	The 'W' formation	73
21.	The 'M' formation	74
22.	The 4–2–4 formation	75
23.	The 4–3–3 formation	76
24.	The 'sweeper'	78

Introduction

While a friend and I were travelling in the U.S.A. recently we stopped at a camp site somewhere in the Rocky Mountains, and began to set up our tent. As we did so we noticed that our neighbour was a swarthy, dark-skinned foreigner and we eyed each other suspiciously. The atmosphere remained a little frigid until my travelling companion and I took out a rubber ball and began to kick it around. At once a friendly grin with a flash of white teeth lit the face of our neighbour; he sauntered across, clapped us on the back, told us he was a Mexican; we happily reminded him that two days previously England had defeated Mexico 2–0 in the World Cup and we spent half that night talking of Carbajal, Charlton and the great game of soccer.

How many other games can claim quite the international appeal that soccer possesses? You have only to recall the remarkable interest in the World Cup—400 million watched the 1966 final on TV; you have only to look at the ever-increasing popularity of the various European Cup competitions, to realize how soccer can cut clean through language barriers and national hostilities. While I was teaching and touring in the U.S.A. I was struck by the growing enthusiasm for soccer there and, in my view, it won't be very long before that great country becomes yet another convert to the most popular team game in the world.

15

Some of you who are reading this book will, I hope, one day enjoy the opportunity to travel through your soccer; and many of you will find that soccer is a game that enables you to make many close friends—at school and when you leave—as well as affording you a lot of fun. Although very few of you will ever become professional footballers, remember that the amateur game provides the real life blood of soccer. In many countries, such as Sweden, Denmark, Holland, Switzerland—all players are amateur, and in England did you know that there are over 44,000 amateur clubs enjoying their soccer every Saturday afternoon? Not to mention the millions who follow the game as spectators, armchair critics, or those who are associated in some way or another with the local club.

Inevitably numerous soccer books and magazines have already added to this expanding interest in the game, and we all enjoy reading the memoirs of the great professional players. But in the following pages I shall be suggesting to you the main ways in which you can improve your own skill as a footballer, and your own understanding of the game. Whatever your present ability, whether you are fast or slow, whether you are in the 1st XI or 3rd XI—my advice is aimed at you. We don't all kick, head or trap a football in exactly the same manner, but there are certain fundamentals that every aspiring footballer must learn. It is these basic principles on which I shall be concentrating. I have intentionally used photographs of schoolboys of 15–17 years—not all boys of outstanding ability—and you will see them attempting various skills (not always with 100 per cent success), skills which are well within your capabilities over the coming years. You will note too, that where possible the boys have been photographed performing such skills as heading, trapping and shooting under pressure (either being challenged or in a match situation). It is all too easy for a defender to trap or for a goalkeeper to save a ball without any challenge—but most unnatural, and we should always aim to connect our practices as closely as possible to what actually happens in a game. You will be able to compare these boys with some professionals photographed demonstrating the same skills. I hope, too, that you will find Chapter 4 helpful in understanding the changing tactics of modern soccer—4–2–4, 4–3–3 etc.; and in Chapter 5 I have laid strong emphasis on the lessons to be learnt by intelligent watching of soccer, a point all too often neglected by young players! And in Chapter 6 I have looked at the lessons to be learnt from the 1970 World Cup series in Mexico.

But do remember one thing. My advice will be of little value to you if you just read this book, look at the photographs and do no more. The more you put into any game, the more you will gain from it. At your age, if you are prepared to practise hard, to overcome your faults, you will not only enjoy your soccer more, you might one day experience the thrill of playing in New York, Moscow or Mexico City.

I

Preparing for the Game

How much do you prepare yourself for a game of football? Do you rush out to play immediately after two helpings of plum pudding? Do you alter your studs according to the state of the ground? Do you train properly? Do you bother about wearing 'shin-pads'?

Obviously the amount of preparation we give to any game depends largely upon the standard at which we are playing. The World Cup Teams can be said to start their preparation up to four years in advance; and at the professional level nowadays— psychologists; physiotherapists; tactical discussions; films of opponents; diets, and a million training routines—all are part of the preparation before a big match. For you at school many of these clearly can't apply, but there are several ways in which you can ensure that you arrive on the field fully equipped to give of your best.

How to Train

It is up to your coach or master-in-charge to encourage and organize your training, but you should be prepared to help to-wards your own fitness by:

1. Working hard at all training routines (photographs 1 & 2).

19

1 and 2. *Working hard in training*. You will notice plenty of determination and concentration in this training session on the Shrewsbury School playing fields.

2. Training on your own if necessary. (Sprint ten yards then walk ten yards, increasing the number of sprints on each training session.)

3. Realizing that all the stamina training in the world is of *no* value unless you ensure that you sleep well before a match.

4. Where possible (and I know that this is sometimes difficult) eating long before kick-off, and so giving your food time to be digested. Alternatively have a light lunch—and fill up on cream buns *after* you have been victorious.

5. Arriving in the changing-room, leaving yourself ample time before the game starts. There is nothing more certain to create panic in a boys' side than a rush before the game and two goals down in the first ten minutes.

6. Warming yourself up properly before the game starts, for you can't play effectively until your muscles and joints are loosened. This is particularly essential on a cold day. Go out on to that pitch ten minutes before the game starts, and don't just stand there kicking the occasional ball at the goalkeeper. A few sprints, a few stretches and twists will do you much more good.

What to Wear

At first sight this might seem unnecessary advice. Isn't it obvious what we wear on the football field?! Yes; but you would be surprised how often your performance suffers because you haven't put on the right boots. I have seen goalkeepers allowing the ball to slither through their hands (because they have forgotten their gloves); players shivering with numb hands (because they have not taken cold weather into account); I have even seen one player tying up his bootlace whilst the opponent he should have been marking calmly scored! You certainly can improve your performance (and your enjoyment) by dressing sensibly:

1. A clean, smart 'strip' does much to make you feel a footballer, and a well turned-out team often makes the opposition feel a little inferior.

2. When you buy a new pair of boots it is usually wise to ask for half a size smaller than your normal shoes—because football boots expand with wear—but try them on and choose carefully. Footballers should treat their boots with loving care; make

quite sure that they are the correct size; break them in gently; clean them regularly; dry them slowly if the ground has been wet, and dubbin them after each game. Ensure that your studs are well suited to the playing conditions. If you wear long studs on a hard ground, your blisters will remind you how foolish you have been; if you wear short studs on a soft surface your bruised backside will do the reminding! So be sensible. If you use screw-in studs, be prepared to change them after you have looked at the ground. Remember, too, that a referee can send you off if you are wearing jagged studs which might cause injury to your opponents.

Most of you, I am sure, do clean your boots before each game, but how many of you tie your laces correctly? The essential point here is to avoid tying the knot in the kicking area of the boot. If possible tie it around the outside of the boot and tuck those loose ends out of sight, as in Figure 1.

3. Shin-pads are not always used by professionals nowadays, but most of them pad their ankles carefully. It is up to you and your coach whether you want to protect your shins or not. Some players feel free without shin-pads, but if you are playing in a

FIG. 1. How to tie your boots

position where tackling is essential (and that means most positions) I would strongly advise wearing a lightweight pad. If you don't, you are sure to suffer sooner or later from a bruised and gashed shin. Not very pleasant, I can assure you!

4. A footballer usually needs something tied around the top of his calf to keep his socks up. A word of warning here—beware of tying too tightly and thus causing cramp (a thin strip of bandage is often preferable to a tight garter).

5. A goalkeeper must remember to have handy his gloves (should it be wet and the ball slithery), and his cap (should he find the sun glaring into his eyes). Also don't be frightened to play in track-suit trousers if the goalmouth is hard and frosty.

6. If the weather is bitterly cold, rub the exposed parts of your body with liniment or Vaseline, and then you will be warm enough to contribute 100 per cent effort on the nastiest days. If you are playing in a very hot climate and perspiring heavily, some salt at half-time will often revitalize you.

2

Improving Your Skill

When you see your favourite players in action, when you rush for their autographs and when you envy the wonderful life of the successful footballer, don't forget all the hard work that goes on behind the scenes. Have you ever realized how hard Pele had to practise to develop his famed right foot; or how much heading practice is essential to reach the standard of a Seeler or a Law? Professional footballers have in many ways completed all their hard work *before* the match begins, in their practice and constant attention to basic skills, their kicking, heading, trapping, etc. Whether you improve your skills with a tennis ball as Sir Stanley Matthews did, in the back streets of your local town, in your school playground, or on your father's lawn—it is all the same. You will never make a footballer unless you are prepared to work at the fundamental arts of the game.

Kicking

We call our game *Foot*ball and if you can't kick you can't become a footballer. If you learn to kick with either foot you will be an infinitely more valuable player than if you kick with one (and use the other merely to stand on!) There are of course different styles of kicking a ball and a slight readjustment of technique is needed for a ball running away from the kicker, or coming from the left or right. If you are in your early teens you cannot yet expect to exert much power, but there are certain fundamental principles in kicking:

(*a*) Keep your eye on the ball.
(*b*) Ensure that you are balanced.
(*c*) Position the non-kicking foot correctly.
(*d*) Follow through with the kicking leg.
(*e*) Aim for accuracy rather than power.

Let us look more closely at the various methods of kicking a football, and we shall discover the importance of these five principles:

1. *Kicking with the instep*

This is probably the most common way of kicking and is valuable when passing and shooting (whether short, long, low or high).

If you look at the photographs 3, 4 and 5 you will clearly see the crucial stages of a low instep pass. Notice the balanced position of 3 and 4, the balance of hands, as well as head; note how the player has his head and knee over the ball, and this, together with the fact that his left foot is placed close to the ball will ensure that the pass is kept low; in 5 you will see that vital follow through (necessary for a longer pass or shot) and notice, too, how the player is still looking at the original position of the ball (rather as a golfer should keep his head down for as long as possible).

If our player had wanted to *loft* his pass or his shot by chipping the ball (as a winger frequently has to do), he would then *not* place his standing foot so close to the ball, but would allow his body to lean back rather than forward and the outcome is excellently demonstrated in photographs 6, 7 and 8. Again note the balanced position of the kicker and you will see that the follow

3

4

Fig. 2. Kicking with the instep

3, 4 and 5. *The low instep pass.* Three stages of this kick. Notice the balanced position, the head and knee over the ball in (3) and (4) and the full follow through in (5).

5

through still occurs. But compare the angle of the body with that of the low kicker. With a lofted kick you will often find it easier to run diagonally at the ball rather than from directly behind it.

2. *Kicking with the inside of the foot*

This type of kick, demonstrated in photograph 9 is probably the most accurate, and should primarily be used for the short pass—on the ground and on the volley. The same principles apply here as with the instep kick. Eye on the ball; standing foot alongside the ball; the knee of the kicking foot over the ball in order to keep the pass low; but the follow through is inevitably more limited. It is more of a sharp jab than a fluent movement.

6

6, 7 and 8. *The lofted pass.* In this case, a centre from the left wing. Look at the position of the standing foot in (6)—*behind the ball.* Compare the angle of the body in (8) with that of the boy in (5).

7

8

9. *Kicking with the inside of the foot*. The most accurate method of making a short pass.

Fig. 3. Kicking with the inside of the foot

3. *Kicking with the outside of the foot*

Ten years ago very few players bothered to kick with the outside of the foot; but the South Americans and the Continentals soon demonstrated its value. If you possess a right foot stronger than your left and therefore find it difficult to pass to your outside right, try using the outside of your strong foot. In addition, it often deceives your opponent if you suddenly flick the ball through with the outside of your foot. Try it. Mind you, you will find it much easier to kick this way if you are pigeon-toed! Study our player at the moment of impact in photograph 10. The ball finished in the bottom right-hand corner of the net!

4. *The backheel*

This can be valuable and unexpected, but remember that it

FIG. 4. Kicking with
the outside of the foot

10. *Kicking with the outside
of the foot.* Hardly what the
goalkeeper expected here!

is always far better *to play the way you are facing.* The backheel is
eye-catching, but in my experience, very rarely effective.

5. *The volley and half-volley*

As you know, the ball spends much of its time in the air (too
much sometimes) and there are many occasions when in defence
you have to volley the ball clear, or when, at centre-forward, you
have to risk a snap shot on the volley (or half-volley)—and a
very difficult skill this is.

However, apply the kicking principles stated above, never
take your eye off the ball and try (even on the volley) to get your
knee over the ball as the boy in photograph 11 has done as he
shoots. Notice again the eye on the ball and the balanced position. In too many cases the volley or half-volley kick soars high
in the air, and it is often wiser to volley a shorter pass using the
inside of the foot.

30

11. *The volley.* A fine action shot of the volley at the moment of impact. Note the balance and concentration. Above all, look at the way the right knee *leads* the right foot in order to keep the volley as low as possible.

6. *The bicycle kick*

When you have conquered these basic methods of kicking try to emulate the brilliant overhead kick (or bicycle kick) demonstrated in photograph 38 in the final chapter. But I advise a well-sprung mattress to fall upon!

Trapping

When we watch a professional footballer controlling a difficult pass don't we sometimes feel that he must have the ball on some invisible string, so well does he take possession of it—with his feet, thighs, chest or head? Yet how often do we find that simple pass bouncing away from us as we attempt to control,

12. *Trapping—with the inside of the foot.* The right foot has just squeezed the ball against the ground. Although the boy is well balanced here, he hasn't quite killed the ball 'dead', has he?
13. *Trapping—with the outside of the foot.* Look at the head, arms and balance here—but see also how the challenging defender is 'screened' from the ball by white's use of his body.

trap or 'kill' the ball? Remember that the more quickly we can control the ball, the more chance we have of passing it accurately before we are tackled, so let us look more closely at the various types of trapping and the technique involved.

The essential point to remember in all forms of stationary trapping is that your body (or whichever part of your body you are using for the trap) must 'give' a little, to cushion the ball just as it is about to make contact. This applies to control with head, foot, chest or thigh. If you look closely at the boys in photographs 12–17, you will see this cushioning effect, but also notice

14. *Trapping—on the volley.* The most common method of controlling the ball.

the eyes concentrating on the ball even though an opponent is challenging closely.

1. *Control with the foot*

There are numerous ways of trapping with the foot and the first one that you should perfect is the simple 'squeeze' trap, which involves controlling the ball between your foot and the ground, using either the sole or the inside of the boot.

Once you have conquered this, try trapping the ball *on the move*, again squeezing it between foot and ground but dragging it to your left or right as you bring it under control. The boy in photograph 12 is showing the value of this trap as he is already on the move before he can be tackled by the opponent waiting to challenge. Try trapping with *the outside* of your foot as well as the inside. You might not find this easy at first but it will help you to move off in either direction.

Often you will find the ball coming towards you at that diffi-

15. *The chest trap—concave.* By leaning forward, the ball will drop from the chest to the player's feet. No, he is *not* handling the ball here!

16. *The chest trap—convex.* Note the difference. Leaning back, cushioning the ball and reaching up off the ground. Excellently demonstrated here, although the arms could be held wider.

cult knee height, and the most effective method of controlling such a ball is to cushion it on the volley with the inside of your foot (as in photograph 14). This is probably the trap most commonly used in the game itself.

2. *Control with other parts of the body*

In addition you will have to learn to control that unpleasant ball which arrives at chest or throat level and, in this case, try cushioning the ball on your chest. There are two equally effective methods of controlling the ball with your chest. Either by the concave trap (photograph 15) or the convex (16), but notice again in both instances the eyes, the use of the body, and the cushioning effect.

17. *The thigh trap.* It looks as if the boy in white is trapping the ball with his stomach, but if you look closely you will see that his right knee is on its way up to cushion the ball. Note also the excellent challenge from the defender—waiting for the slightest slip.

Finally, as you become more confident in your control, try trapping the ball on the head (cushion it again), on the thigh (as in photograph 17) or cradle it in the instep as it drops. If you really work upon these methods of trapping and control, you will in time discover that you are able to accept all types of passes with complete confidence. But it will take a lot of practice!

Heading

We have just seen how the head can be used to trap or cushion the high ball, and a good footballer should be able to head the ball as confidently, accurately and (almost) as powerfully as he can kick it.

The basic principles of heading are quite clear:

(a) Eyes on the ball.

18. *Heading—the simple pass.* Just before the moment of impact. Note the eyes.

19. *Jumping and heading.* Although he hasn't headed the ball, the boy in white has prevented the tall defender (in dark strip) from placing his header unchallenged.

20. *The defensive header.* Notice the power, the leap, but also the follow through of the head.

18

(*b*) Use the forehead. (You will soon realize that the remainder of your head does not approve of the hard thud of a football.)

(*c*) Head from the hips, *not* just by waggling the head itself. Power stems from the waist.

(*d*) Time your spring, when jumping to head.

If you look at photograph 18 you will see the simple, straight headed pass. Notice the concentration and balance again, and the potential power as our player waits to head the ball. But remember that in a game you will have very little chance to stand still and head the ball; you will almost certainly be challenged in the air, often by someone larger than yourself and this is where the timing of your jump is crucial. You must reach upwards *yet still keep your eyes on the ball.* This isn't always easy, as the two boys in photograph 19 show. They have jumped well, but are they watching that ball? By contrast in photograph 20 you can clearly see a fine demonstration of a strong defensive header. The boy in the dark colours, though challenged, has

36

19

20

leapt high, watched the ball and has headed powerfully.

Heading sideways (or backwards) is, of course, more difficult than a straight header, but you still use the forehead (*not* the left ear or the back of the head as many boys do!), and turn from the hips.

There are two other points worth remembering. It is easier to head the ball upwards rather than downwards, but, if you are a forward you will trouble the opposing goalkeeper far more if you aim at his knees—as the player in photograph 21 is attempting to do. But compare this schoolboy header with photograph 22. Here we see Bene (of Hungary) in a World Cup match *v*. Bulgaria demonstrating all the power and accuracy of a header at goal. Note the downward trajectory of the ball, the stretching neck and the eyes still riveted on the ball. Finally it doesn't matter how small you are; if you challenge your taller opponent for a header, even if you don't make contact you will prevent him from having a 'free' headed pass. Don't stand and watch.

21, 22. *The header at goal.* Both players here are heading *downwards*—far more difficult for a goalkeeper to save. The school-boy (*above*), though challenged, has directed his header intelligently. But look at the perfect downward header by Bene of Hungary (*below*) as he defeats Simonov in a 1966 World Cup match between Hungary and Bulgaria.

23, 24. *The block tackle.* Compare these two photographs and you will see how much more chance the defender (in the dark colours) has of winning the ball in (23) than in (24) *because his weight is in the tackle.*

Tackling

Increasingly in the modern game of football you will discover that players are coached to 'hold off' the tackle, to back away from the opponent with the ball, and I shall refer to this tactic in the next chapter. But this does *not* mean that tackling is a disappearing skill. Far from it—it remains a vital one, especially for defenders and especially in and around the penalty box. You must never forget that football *is* a physical game and all the pretty ball control in the world is of little value unless you are prepared to meet a tackle, challenge or do the tackling yourself.

There are three important points to remember when tackling:
(*a*) The timing of your tackle. (It is no good rushing at an opponent from five yards away. Move closer and wait until he is off balance.)

39

(*b*) Watch the ball (not your opponent's feet!).

(*c*) Where possible ensure that your full weight is over the ball when you tackle. (Even if you are a lightweight you will be surprised how often you can dispossess a heavier opponent if you put your whole weight into the tackle.)

Let us look briefly at the main ways of tackling.

1. *Block tackle*

This, demonstrated in photograph 23, is the most common method of tackling, and you will notice how effectively the defender (in blue) is about to bring his weight into the tackle. Note the contrast in photograph 24 where he is leaning away from the tackle and is far less likely to win the ball.

2. *Sliding tackle*

Many defenders favour this tackle, especially on a wet ground, and if *timed properly*, as in photograph 25, it can be most effective. But remember that if you fail to make contact with this tackle you will be left stranded on the ground while your opponent moves happily forward.

There are, of course, variations on these tackles, and photograph 26 is an excellent example of one of these, but the same principles apply. This tackle by Harris (Chelsea) on Ford (Sheffield Wednesday) in an F.A. Cup Tie portrays all the strength, timing and balance of the perfect tackle. Above all notice the fierce concentration and determination of both players.

While we are talking of physical contact in football don't neglect the fair shoulder charge (shoulder to shoulder), often very effective if delivered while your opponent has the ball. Finally never feel that tackling is 'a defender's job'; you forwards will be far more valuable to your team if you are willing to tackle back and know how to tackle!

25. *The sliding tackle*. Often effective on a wet surface.

26. *The professional tackle*. Look at the power and timing in this splendid action shot.

Dribbling

The days of the great dribblers—the Matthews and the Finneys—seem to be over, and the modern game of football lays more stress on functional team work than individual genius. But football would be far less exciting without the dribbling of such players as Best, Johnstone and Eusebio and if you possess the ability to dribble you can still be a key member of your team. What distinguishes the dribbler?

(*a*) Ball control.

(*b*) A change of speed (the ability to dribble slowly at a defender and then to accelerate past him).

(*c*) The ability to dodge, swerve and turn (with the ball, of course).

(*d*) A natural feint (Each dribbler has his own brand of feint; but whether yours is a shrug of the shoulders, or a shuffle of the feet you must aim to send your opponent 'the wrong way', 'sell him the dummy'.)

If you have this natural feint and this change of speed, do develop it, but if possible practise against another boy. Dribbling in and out of sticks is far too unnatural to be of any great value. But remember, finally, that although a dribbler often catches the eye, he can hold on to the ball too long—and a quick accurate pass is often better than all the dribbling in the world.

Screening

This is an important technique that has been introduced to the game of football over the past 20 years, principally by the Europeans. 'Screening' involves protecting the ball by placing your body between it and your opponent. It is especially valu-

27. *Screening*. The ball is concealed from the defender (dark colours) by the body of the boy in white.

able when dribbling and trapping but often we screen the ball without realizing it. The boys in photographs 12–17 are doing just this, for, as they trap, their body is protecting the ball from the challenging opponent. But photograph 27 shows more clearly how you can make it very difficult indeed for an opponent to tackle by keeping your body between him and the ball. Remember that it is almost impossible to make a fair tackle from behind.

Throw-In

This paragraph applies primarily to wing-halves—but there will be occasions when a full-back or a wing-forward (for instance) will need to take a quick throw-in, and you should all know how to carry out this skill. If you look at photograph 28 you will clearly see the important principles applied:

(*a*) The thrower must deliver the ball from over his head.

(*b*) Both hands must be used.

(*c*) As you throw, both feet must remain touching the ground.

(*d*) You must, of course, *not* be inside the touchline when you throw in, though you can be on it.

Far too often boys break these straightforward rules—so make sure you don't. You can throw with your feet one behind the other—like the boy in the photograph—or you can place your feet side by side, but a run up of a few yards will often give you a longer throw. (If you possess a long throw, work on it and develop it, because you can often cause great concern with a throw into the opposing penalty area.) Remember, too, that a quick throw-in taken by the nearest player is often far more rewarding than waiting for your wing-half to run 30 yards, by which time everyone is probably closely marked.

28. *The throw-in.* Ready to unleash a long throw. Note the use of the body here.

44

Individual Practices

There are a million ways by which you can improve your personal skill with a football, and no doubt your schoolmasters, your coaches or you yourselves have discovered various valuable practices, including some of the suggestions I am about to make at the end of this chapter. It is relatively simple to practise heading, trapping and so on when you have two or three friends with you (and there are a lot of books on soccer which will give you ideas), but not so easy when you are on your own; and I shall concentrate on individual practice in the following section.

1. *Goalkeeper*

Using a firm wall, drop kick the ball from 5 to 10 yards away and immediately prepare yourself to save the rebound. A white blob (or chalked circle) in the centre of the wall can be used for accuracy; and from a greater distance of 20 to 30 yards, you goalkeepers can profitably practise your throwing, again aiming at a given target.

2. *Screening*

Dribble the ball against an imaginary opponent, constantly changing the position of your body in order to protect the ball. You can use the trees in your garden as imaginary opponents, or, even better, if you possess a lively dog try screening the ball from him!

3. *Kicking and Controlling*

There is no better practice than kicking the ball (it doesn't matter whether it is a tennis ball, beach ball or football; in fact, the smaller the better) against a wall of any description, and controlling the rebound. This is how many of the great players improved their control, and there are many possibilities. You can have a contest between your right and left foot; count the number of times you strike the white circle (or any mark) on the wall. Why not chalk or mark several circles, with the bull's eye in the centre offering additional points, and see what you score in twenty attempts? Next time you are on your own with a ball, try to better your record score. There are endless possibilities, and you are not only having fun, you are improving your kicking and controlling skills. Two final words of warning however. *Never* use your hands in these private contests and mind your father's (and the neighbours') windows!

4. *Heading*

It is more difficult to improve your heading without the assistance of other players, but there is some value in seeing how many times you can keep the ball up on your head. This helps

FIG. 5. Practise heading on your own

46

29. *Practise on your own.* Keep the ball on the volley as many times as you can. The younger you start, the better.

your balance, but it isn't related to the sort of heading we need in a game itself. Better, then, if you can set up a football dangling on a firm piece of cord, securely attached to the branch of a tree (or some such 'anchor'). If this ball is hanging at the right height (just above your head) you can find some valuable and enjoyable practice, jumping to head the swinging ball and improve your timing and your heading skill.

5. *Trapping and Control*

As with heading you will find it helpful to your ball control to see how many times you can keep the ball up consecutively on the volley. Then try it with left foot and then the right foot alone. Keep a record and try to beat your best score each time you practice. You can improve your trapping simply by throwing the ball up in the air or against the wall and cushioning it as it comes down; but to give yourself some 'competition' draw a circle—fairly large at first, if you like—on the ground and set up a number of skittles outside the circle, so that if you fail to trap the ball correctly it will bounce out of the circle, knocking over the skittles. Keep a score of how many skittles you disturb while attempting twenty traps, and, again, come back and beat your record another day.

These are only suggestions, only a start at improving your skill with a football, and you will soon discover many variations on these themes. The best practice of all is to find yourself a six-a-side game—it doesn't matter how organized, or whether it is played in the street, on a proper ground or on the sand by the sea; here is the time to put into practice all the skills that you have been learning on your own and all the skills we have covered in this chapter.

3

Positional Play

In the last few years soccer has changed so much that we can no longer talk about the forwards doing all the attacking, while only the halves and full-backs defend. You have probably seen full-backs scoring goals (in their opponent's net!) and forwards packing their own goalmouth. Numbers on players' shirts now mean far less, and many professional clubs in this country are now adopting the European practice of numbering players differently. In fact the game of soccer has become much more fluid—and therefore more exciting.

Nevertheless the duties of individual players, whether they are called 'strikers', 'link-men' or 'sweepers', remain fundamentally the same as ever. Whether you see yourself as a 'Bobby Charlton' or a 'Jim Baxter' the following positional tips still apply:

Goalkeeper

1. *Handling the ball*

Perhaps the first essential of any young goalkeeper is a safe pair of hands. It is all very well making a spectacular looking save—but the best goalkeepers are those who *catch* the ball when it is possible to do so. If you look at photographs 30, 31, 32 you will see three of the most effective methods of catching the ball.

Three ways of catching the ball

30. *Catching the chest-high drive.* Note the hands enveloping the ball and the goalkeeper off the ground in order to take the ball at a comfortable height.

31. *Catching the ball.* Hands behind the ball, feet well off the ground. But if closely challenged, instead of catching it, tip such a high ball as this over the crossbar.

32. *Catching the low ball.* The vital point here is that the body *must* be behind the ball.

Notice:

(*a*) The hands *behind* the ball.

(*b*) The eyes on the ball.

(*c*) The body in line behind the shot.

If you neglect these golden rules you will all too frequently allow the ball to squeeze past you into the net—or allow an opponent to follow up and score when you fail to hold on to a strong shot.

2. *Punching clear*

Of course you won't always be able to catch the fiercest or

33. *The two-fisted punch.* Although the centre-forward is challenging well here, the goalkeeper has kept his eye on the ball and punched decisively. Incidentally, note the good cover by the full-back on the goal line.

cleverest shots. On such occasions, if in doubt, it is often safest to flip the ball over the cross bar or round the post. *Never palm the ball straight up in the air.* For if you do you might make yourself popular with the opposing forwards, but not with your own defenders! If you are forced to punch the ball clear (when jumping with a tall opponent for instance) make sure that you *keep your eye on the ball* (again!) that arms are straight, not bent, and that you punch as demonstrated so well in photograph 33. Two fists are safer than one, though as you grow more experienced you might find, as some professionals do, that you prefer punching with one.

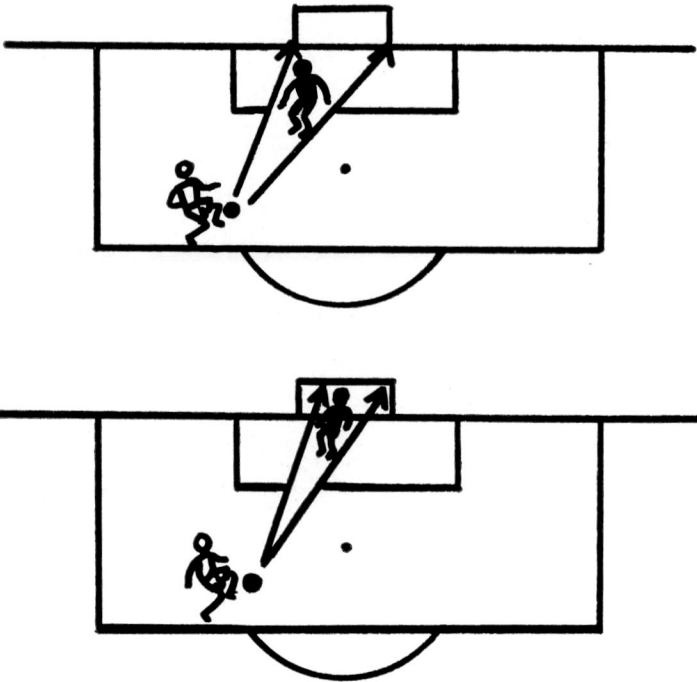

FIGS. 6, 7. Goalkeeper narrowing the angle. Note the
Contrast above

3. *Narrowing the angle*

This is one of the most difficult aspects of goalkeeping, and
you will only learn with constant practice. However good the
defence in front of you, there will be times when an opposing
forward is through; and if you look at Figures 6 and 7 you will
see how much simpler is the forward's job of scoring if you stay
on your goal-line; and how much less of the goal is visible if you
move out to 'narrow the angle'. One of the vital rules for any
goalkeeper is to make up his mind rapidly whether to come out
or stay on his line, and this applies to centres and corners as well
as through passes. Watch how much of the penalty area a goal-

Goalkeeper diving at a forward's feet

34. Here we see a schoolboy goalkeeper bravely smothering a short-range shot. Note how the body covers the goal.

35. Yashin (U.S.S.R.) diving successfully at the feet of Seeler (W. Germany) in a 1966 World Cup semi-final. Note how securely the ball is guarded.

keeper like Bonnetti (Chelsea) covers when he makes up his mind to come out.

4. *Diving at a forward's feet*

Any good goalkeeper needs to be courageous—no more so than when he is called upon to dive at the feet of a threatening opponent. It is perfectly safe and most effective if you remember:

(*a*) To keep your eye on the ball.

(*b*) *Not* to dive in head first!

There are two main methods of going down at a forward's feet, demonstrated by a young goalkeeper in photograph 34 and by the great Yashin (Russia) in 35 as he goes down at the feet of

Seeler (West Germany) in the 1966 World Cup. Look at them closely; they are both saving 'certain' goals!

5. *Distribution and Kicking*

A goalkeeper is the last line of defence, it is true. But we mustn't forget that he is also the first line of attack; and the best goalkeepers often set their attack in motion with a long kick to a fast breaking forward, or a quick throw to an unmarked colleague. Obviously, if you have a strong centre-forward in your team, a long kick for him to head on (especially with the wind behind you) is thoroughly sensible. But try to get into the habit of *throwing* a pass when possible—it is a far more constructive way of building an attack, as long as the throw is *quick* and *low*. In addition far too many school goalkeepers are poor kickers of the ball, and tend to leave goal-kicks to their full-backs. Don't make the same mistake—a goalkeeper who can kick is a real asset to his team.

6. *Calling*

A final (and often neglected) tip to a goalkeeper concerns calling to defenders. Frequently you, in goal, are the only player who can see the whole play developing in front of you, and a shout of, 'Watch your winger, Jim,' or, 'Your ball, Mike,' or, 'Goalkeeper's ball!' will often come as grateful relief to the rest of your defence.

Full-Backs

The basic requirements in any potential full-back are:
(*a*) Speed.
(*b*) Quickness on the turn.
(*c*) Ability to time a tackle.

54

If you possess these qualities you have the makings of a good full-back; positional play and constructive ideas can be built on these foundations. Full-backs such as Cooper (Leeds) and Lawler (Liverpool) frequently appear in important attacking roles in their club teams and do you remember that wonderful goal scored by Gemmell for Celtic in that 1967 European Cup Final? But let us not put the cart before the horse. You must learn to defend before you can consider emulating the professionals.

1. *Positional play*

Much will depend upon what system your school or club team uses, but any full-back should aim to cover his centre-half when the opposition is attacking down the far side of the field. Notice the position of our left-back (LB) in Figure 8, and you will see how he can save the situation if his right-back (or centre-half) is beaten.

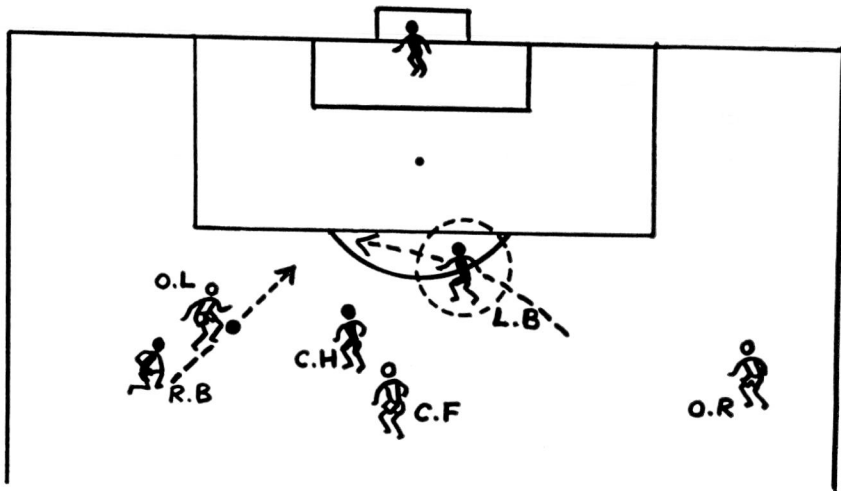

Fig. 8. Positional play of a full-back

55

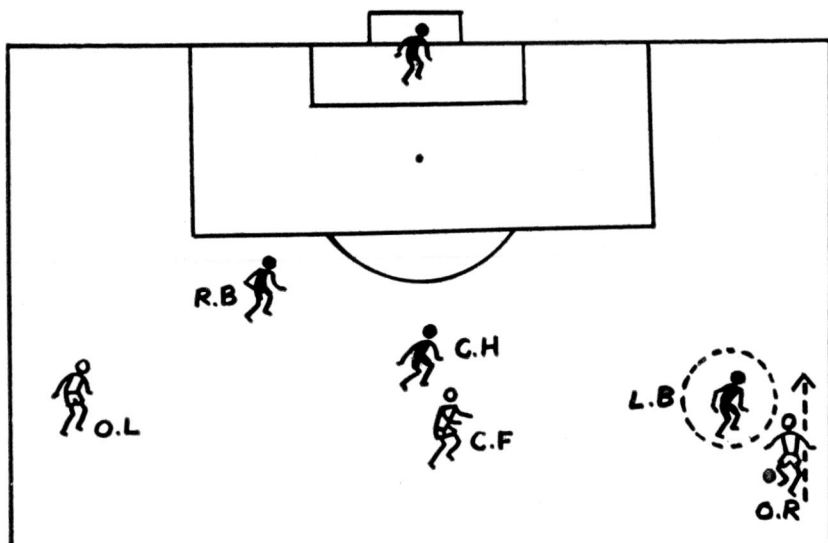

FIG. 9. Positional play of a full-back

Look now at Figure 9, and you will appreciate the different positioning of our L.B. when play is developing on *his* side of the field. He must 'make contact' with the winger who has the ball, standing close enough to crowd the opponent; close enough to tackle should his winger lose control, but far enough away to ensure that the opponent doesn't sprint past him. Many full-backs are now encouraged to follow the opposing winger deep into his own territory—and if you have the speed this can often upset your opponent. Whatever position you play it is wise to try to put yourself in your opponent's place and to say to yourself (for instance): 'Now, what would I like least if I were a winger—having my opposing full-back two yards from me, or ten yards away?'

2. *'Jockeying' or 'Containing' an opponent*
    Having considered the basic positional tactics of full-back

FIG. 10. Defender 'containing' an attacker

play, the next important lesson, the art of 'jockeying' or 'containing' a winger (by this we mean backing away at two or three yards' distance from an opponent who has the ball as in Figure 10) is essential not only for full-backs, but for all defenders. Far too often young full-backs dash courageously, but recklessly into a tackle in mid-field, miss the ball and leave fellow defenders in trouble. Much better to 'contain' your opponent, back away (as far as the edge of the penalty area), watch the ball and then you are not only allowing your colleagues time to funnel back, but enticing your opponent to dribble too far.

One further piece of advice. If you are much stronger with one foot than the other (and most of us are!) always aim to force your dribbling winger to try to pass you on your *strong* side. Note how our full-back in Figure 11 is turning his body in order to bring his right foot (his strong foot) into the impending tackle.

3. *Constructive play*

Having stopped his man, a good full-back will always try to

Fɪɢ. 11. Defender 'containing' an attacker

set his own attack underway and accurate passing is essential here. Yet, increasingly full-backs today are encouraged to 'overlap' their own wingers, move down the touchline, becoming temporarily wingers themselves (look at Figure 12); this sudden appearance of an additional forward can be most helpful, but when you set off on such an attacking run you must ensure:

(*a*) That someone else is dropping back to cover you.

(*b*) That you recover quickly when your attack breaks down.

Centre-Half

There are three outstanding essentials required by a centre-half:

(*a*) Height (for heading power).

(*b*) Calmness (a centre-half's influence is vital).

(*c*) Strength in the tackle.

Speed is not such a necessity for a centre-half and there are of course good, small pivots, but a tall defender who is an effective

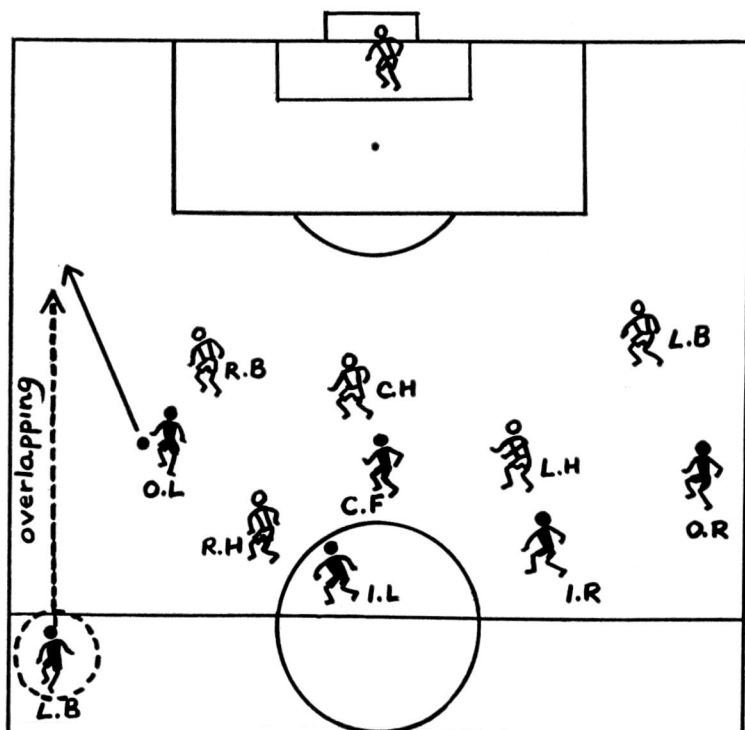

FIG. 12. Overlapping

header of the ball is most helpful in dealing with those high centres. If you look at professional soccer you will find most clubs have a Jack Charlton or Mike England blocking the central path to goal.

Positional play: The centre-half is inevitably the hub of any defence; a central figure around whom full-backs and wing-halves should revolve, and this is why it is such an excellent position from which to captain the side. If you are a centre-half, your first duty will normally entail marking the centre-forward and

59

the same technique in marking applies here as to the full-back (see above):

(a) *Keep on goal side of your opponent.*
(b) *Contain* or *jockey* him until you reach the penalty area (or the danger zone).
(c) Try to force him on to your strong tackling foot.

But there are one or two added problems for a centre-half. How far should he follow a centre-forward who wanders to the wings? Should he mark a 'deep-lying' centre-forward closely or let him go? Is the 'off-side' trap a good idea? These are basically problems that your team coach or master-in-charge must decide upon. If you are playing a 'man-to-man' marking system (see Chapter 4) then you should follow that centre-forward wherever he goes; and if you are playing an 'off-side' game you must ensure that *all* your defenders are fully aware of this, or the results may be fatal. Two further tips to a budding centre-half: if you are strong in the air you can be a valuable force in the opposing penalty area at corners; from centre-half your best constructive passes are often to your wingers who are usually easier to find from your central position than the other forwards.

Wing-Halves

We can divide our wing-halves nowadays into the defensive half-back (or double centre-half) and the attacking half-back (or 'link man'); but whichever role you favour, the basic requirements are much the same:

(a) *Stamina* and *strength.*
(b) *Constructive ability.*
(c) *Marking ability.*

Even in the modern, fluid patterns of soccer any wing-half *must* possess the determination and capacity for hard work throughout the whole game. No team can succeed without strong wing-halves. Do you remember how Mackay and Blanchflower made the great Spurs side of 1960–4 tick; did you realize the value of Stiles and Crerand in the success of Manchester United?

Positional play: Before you read the next two paragraphs remember that the best half-backs are those who can perform defensive and attacking 'roles'. At your age it is a mistake to concentrate on one at the expense of the other.

1. *Defensive wing-half*

Many of his positional requirements are similar to those of a centre-half, and the ability to mark an opponent closely is more important here than the ability to construct. If you are primarily a defensive half-back, you should be positioned alongside your centre-half and your main duty involves watching and marking the most thrustful of the opposing inside-forwards (see L.H. on Figure 13)—so stay on your goal side of this potential goal-scorer; *don't* get drawn too far up-field; and make sure you have a good understanding with your centre-half. (See also the comments in the next chapter on 'the sweeper'.)

2. *Attacking wing-half*

As an attacking wing-half you should always be in the game; pushing up field behind your forwards, moving back to mark an opponent when your attack breaks down, and collecting the ball out of defence to set your forwards away again. An attacking wing-half needs stamina and intelligence—and the best attacking half-backs are *not* necessarily those who dribble the ball up-field; *but those who give a quick, constructive and accurate pass* to their forwards.

Here are three further tips to you, young wing-halves:

Fig. 13. The double centre-half. You can see how much more difficult it is for the I.L. to make a through pass

(*a*) An attacking wing-half is frequently more valuable just behind his forwards rather than amongst them.

(*b*) The long, crossfield pass (right-half to left-wing) is still an excellent one for switching the point of your attack.

(*c*) If you possess a strong shot, make use of it from the edge of the penalty area. Far too many boys nowadays try to walk the ball into the net.

Wing-Forwards

In the modern game of soccer you will see many teams playing with no orthodox wingers at all. (Do you remember the England and Portugal 1966 World Cup sides?). But in schoolboy and junior football, whether we call him a winger or a striker, someone thrusting down the touchline is essential. Perhaps the main requirements of a winger are:

(*a*) Speed.
(*b*) Dribbling ability.
(*c*) Intelligent centring.

It has often been maintained that a winger can survive without needing to head the ball properly, without using the 'weak' foot, and without needing to work as hard as other members of the team. There is some truth in this, but increasingly wingers must be prepared to take on the functions of their colleagues and you will be a far more helpful outside right if you can head, kick with your left foot and give 100 per cent effort in every match.

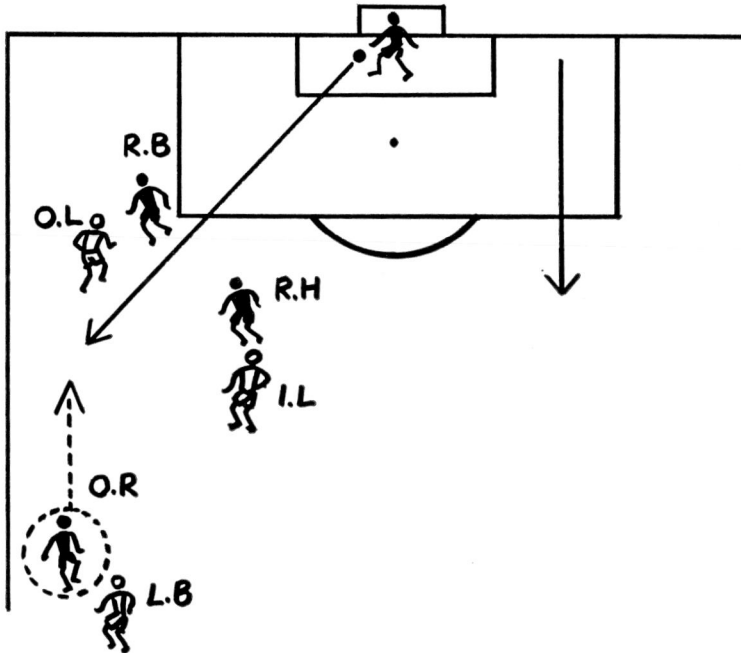

Fig. 14. Positional play of a winger. Colours outside right is here coming deep to receive a pass from his goalkeeper

63

Positional play: As I have suggested in the last paragraph a wing-forward is no longer expected merely to wait for the ball to come to him, sprint down the touchline and centre. You must be prepared to come well back, deep into your own half to collect the ball (see Figure 14); you must chase and mark your opposing full-back if he decides to move upfield; you must move in to the edge of the penalty area when your team-mate on the other wing is about to centre. Possibly the most important aspect of a winger's game is his crossing or centring of the ball. Far too many young players just kick the ball hopefully in the direction of the opposing goalkeeper. This is often pointless—and very popular with the opposition. There are however three types of centre that the opposing goalkeeper dreads:

(*a*) The chip (aimed at the penalty spot) that curls *away* from him.

(*b*) The deep centre over the heads of the defence to the far post (the sort of centre that Hurst of England or Torres of Portugal so enjoyed in the 1966 World Cup).

(*c*) The low 'pull-back' from the goal-line, which often catches the defence off balance and is especially advisable if your forward line is a small one. (See Figure 15 (a), (b) and (c)).

Three final tips for the young winger: *stay as wide as you can,* for by 'hugging' your touch-line you are stretching the opposing defence and giving your inside-forwards more room. Always try to 'run' your opposing full-back early on—discover whether you are faster than he is. A right-footed winger can often be very effective on the left wing—try it!

Inside-Forwards

Some of the greatest names in soccer are those of inside-forwards; Pele, Eusebio, Law, Charlton, Suarez, Albert—one could go on and on. Certainly if you are an inside-forward, you

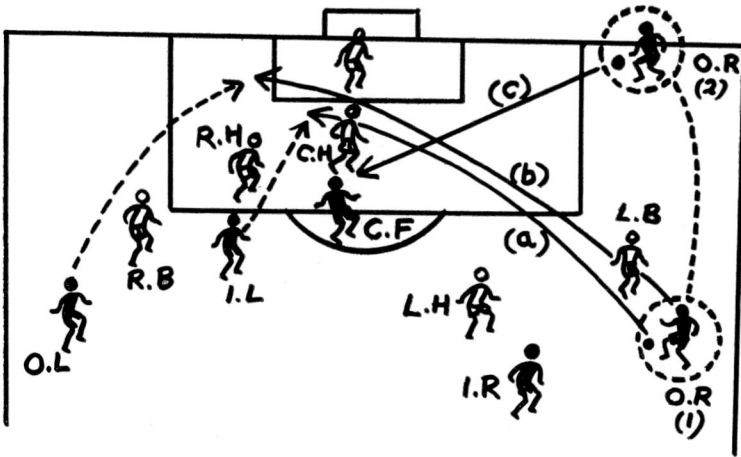

FIG. 15. Wingers—the centre. (a) The O.R. is curling his centre away from the goalkeeper. (b) The long centre for O.L. running in. (c) The pull-back from the goal-line

must be a jack-of-all-trades. Ball control, constructive ability, stamina and hard work, speed and the eye for an opening, tackling back and scoring goals—all these talents go to make up the ideal inside-forward. Do you possess them all?

Positional play: As in the case of wing-halves, so with inside-forwards we often nowadays refer to 'thrusting' or attacking players or to 'deep-lying' constructive ones. The strong, tall hard-shooting inside often acts as a double centre-forward (Hunt of Liverpool, or Hurst of West Ham were typical examples in England's 1966 World Cup success); while the more fragile, delicate ball-player (e.g. McCalliog or Hope) constructs from mid-field. But you will be a better inside-forward if you can carry out *both* these functions. Are Pele, Eusebio, Charlton or Albert just strikers or just creators?—*no*, they are all-purpose inside-forwards.

The positional play of any inside-forward depends to a large

E

FIG. 16. Passes of the inside-forward. Look for the through
pass (c) before any other

extent on team tactics, but here is some advice which applies
whatever your team 'system':

(a) Your main duty is to link your defence and attack, to collect the ball from defence and set your forwards moving.

(b) Always challenge for a high ball in mid-field—even if
your opposing wing-half is much taller than you, never
give him a free head of the ball.

(c) Play the way you are facing. Of course an inside-forward

66

has to be able to turn with the ball, but all too often young players turn straight into an opponent, when a pass can be 'layed-off' to a colleague—*even if you are passing towards your own goal.* It is frequently wise in soccer to move backwards in order to go forwards!

(d) An inside-forward can (and must) be prepared to give the square pass, back pass, cross-field pass and through pass (see Figure 16)—and often the correct pass is obvious. But young insides must always remember that, if it is 'on', *the through ball,* the penetrating pass is always the one that worries the opposing defence most. You ask any defender!

(e) Always think a move ahead. When the ball is on its way to your centre-forward take up a position where you can best help him (see Figure 18).

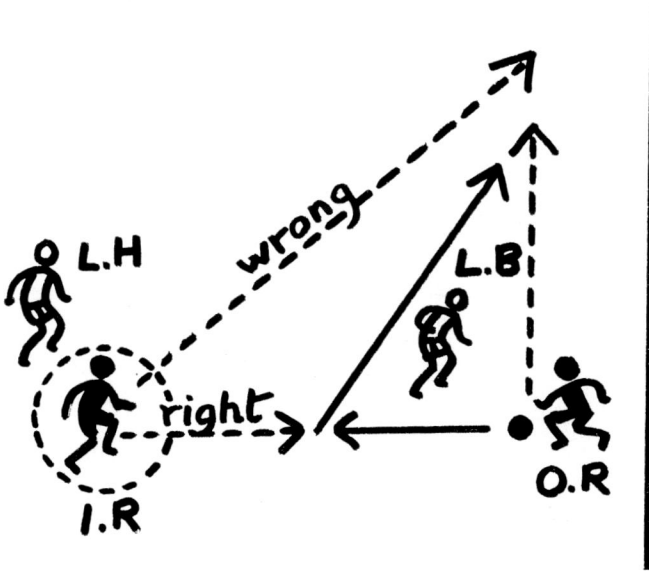

FIG. 17. Positional play of the inside-forward. Note how the I.R. can help his O.R. get behind the full-back

(*f*) Help your winger by moving square with him when he is receiving the ball. (Unless he is fond of cutting in, you will *not* assist him by running into the vacant space ahead of him.) (See Figure 17.)

(*g*) As an inside-forward you are primarily an attacker, but you must help your defence when the opposition gains possession by 'shadowing' and marking your opposing wing-half—especially if he is a forceful, attacking player himself.

Centre-Forward

As centre-forward you might perhaps envisage yourself as the popular goal-scorer, posing dramatically as you dive to score in front of hordes of camera-men! But, in truth, a centre-forward's life is a tough and demanding one if he is doing his full job. Certainly he is expected to score goals, although the 'deep-lying' centre-forward (such as Hideguti in the great Hungarian team of the 1950's), has introduced a more constructive role in recent years. But in addition to a strong shot, and an eye for goal, a good centre-forward needs great courage and determination. Whether you be challenging a tall centre-half in the air, awaiting a fierce defensive tackle as you try to dribble through, or merely chasing those forlorn long passes that reach the opposing goalkeeper long before you arrive—you need a big heart, plenty of fight and must be prepared to do a lot of unselfish running *without the ball.*

Positional play: The new, fluid tactical formations of modern soccer have altered (and often widened) the role of the centre-forward; but if you are a 'central striker' (whether you have number 8, 9 or 10 on your back) you must be mobile, prepared to play backwards, sideways and forwards.

68

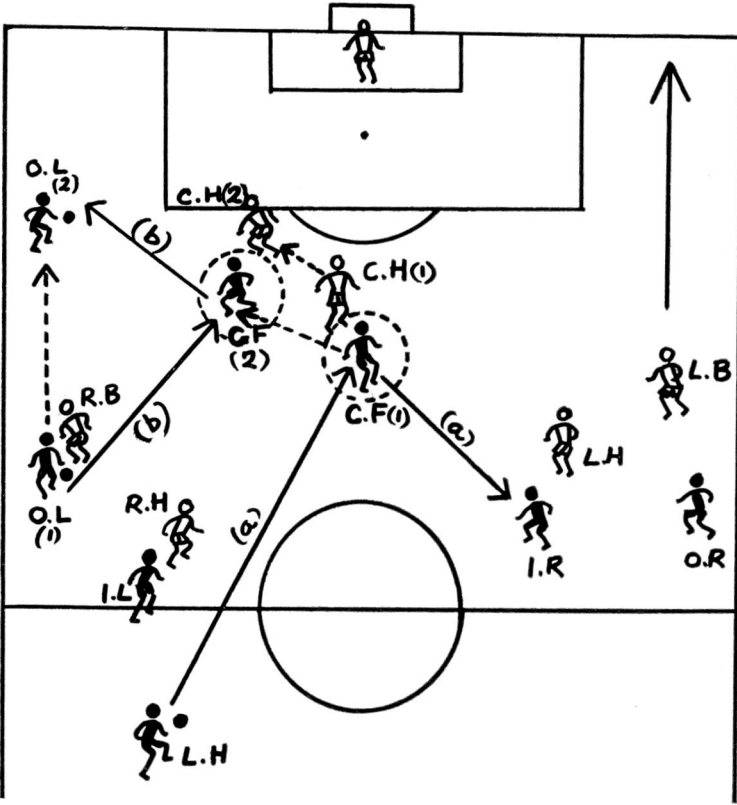

FIG. 18. Positional play of the centre-forward. C.F. (1) is linking up with his L.H. and I.R., C.F. (2) is assisting his O.L.

(a) Backwards

A centre-forward should 'hold' his forward line together, by acting as the pivotal centre of his attack, by linking up with his winger (as in Figure 18 (b)) or by receiving passes from his defence (as in Figure 18 (a)) and laying the ball back to his inside-forward. Notice in both these examples how the centre-forward is *facing his own goal*, keeping his body between the opposing centre-half and the ball (screening), and remember that on all

69

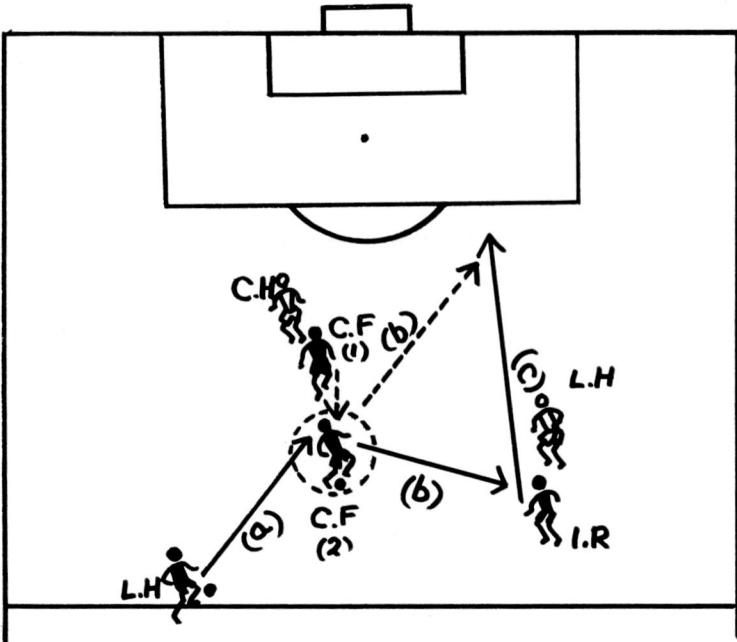

Fig. 19. Positional play of the centre-forward. Notice how the C.F. gives himself more space by coming to meet the pass from his L.H.

36. *'Laying-off' a pass*. Though challenged, the centre-forward turns a first-time pass back to his inside-forward.

these occasions it is vital for a marked forward to *move towards the ball*. (Photograph 36 clearly demonstrates a centre-forward, although closely marked, laying the ball back to his inside-forward.)

(b) Sideways

As centre-forward you should be prepared to move across the field, and by taking your opposing centre-half out to the wing, you will be leaving a valuable vacant space for another forward to exploit. Remember what we said about unselfishness.

(c) Forwards

Naturally the most valuable task for you young centre-forwards is to penetrate, to run for 'through balls', to dribble through and shoot; but you will increasingly find, against well organized defences, that if you attempt to run through all the time, the centre-half's job will be much easier than if you vary your game. How much more effective it is to draw your centre-half up towards the half-way line (see Figure 19), as you receive a pass from your defence, lay the ball off to your inside-forward, and *then* turn and sprint for the through pass.

One final tip. Although centre-forwards dream of scoring by beating three men in a mazy dribble, followed by a superb 30-yard rocket of a shot, remember that most goals (especially at school) are scored by your pouncing upon a 'half-chance' in the penalty area. So always chase and harry in the opposing penalty area. Anyone in my team who is seen standing still in the opposition penalty area (or ours for that matter), is immediately fined a shilling!

4

Understanding the Game

An introduction to tactics

I wonder whether your team uses an orthodox formation or not? Have you a 'sweeper' or an 'overlapping' full-back? Do you really understand the difference between a 4–2–4, and 4–3–3 tactical formation? No doubt your coach or your master-in-charge of football has explained some of these terms and tactics to you, but it is my experience that boys (and adults!) too often use these terms and adopt these tactics without ever grasping their full implications. But before we look at some elementary tactics, never forget that *tactics and formations should be moulded around the individual players*—NOT *vice-versa*.

Team Formations

1. *The 'W' formation*

For many years European and English football has been dominated by the 'W' formation. As Figure 20 shows, this entails two 'W's, one in attack and one in defence. What it really means is that the two inside-forwards play behind the other forwards, and that the two wing-halves move out ahead of their centre-half and full-backs. Obviously there are many variations on this formation. The deep-lying centre-forward, often leading to two thrusting inside-forwards and the wingers coming deeper, has

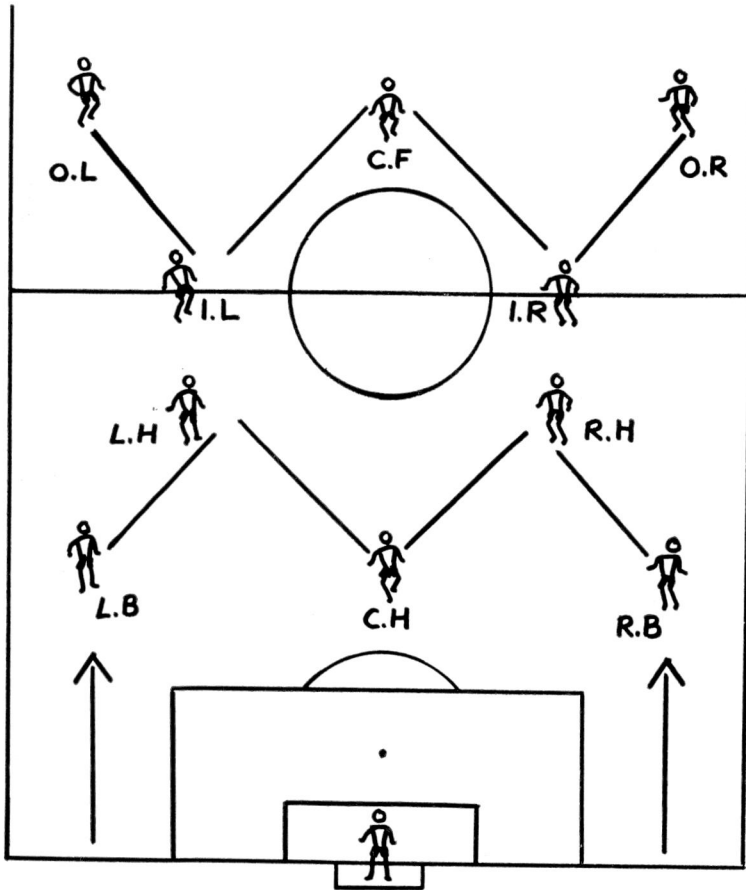

FIG. 20. The 'W' formation

led to the inverted 'W' system (see Figure 21) used so well by Manchester City with Don Revie in 1960. In fact most teams still base their play on these 'W' fundamentals even today. But if your team is opposed by two central strikers (what we call a double centre-forward), you must pull back one of your wing-halves and make him virtually a second centre-half. Likewise in

73

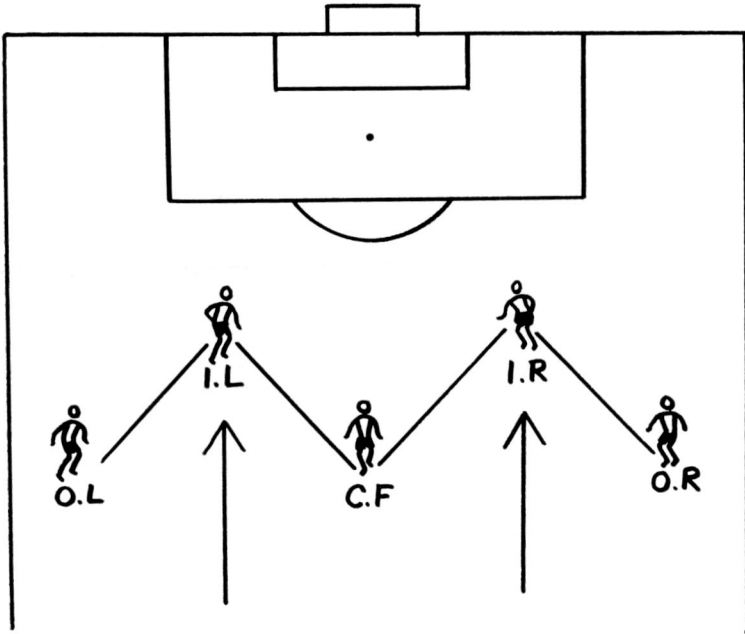

FIG. 21. The 'M' formation

the forward line, if in your team you possess a small, ball-playing inside-forward and a faster, stronger boy with a good kick, then you (or your coach) would be silly to stick rigidly to the 'W' formation, and it would be only sensible to play one inside-forward up and one back. This leads us to our second tactical formation.

2. *The 4–2–4 formation*

Ever since it was introduced by Brazil in the 1958 World Cup, 4–2–4 has been a most popular team system, and certainly provides a strong defensive barrier. As Figure 22 makes clear, it consists of a defensive unit of four (full-backs, centre-half and a defensive wing-half); two 'link' men in midfield (normally an

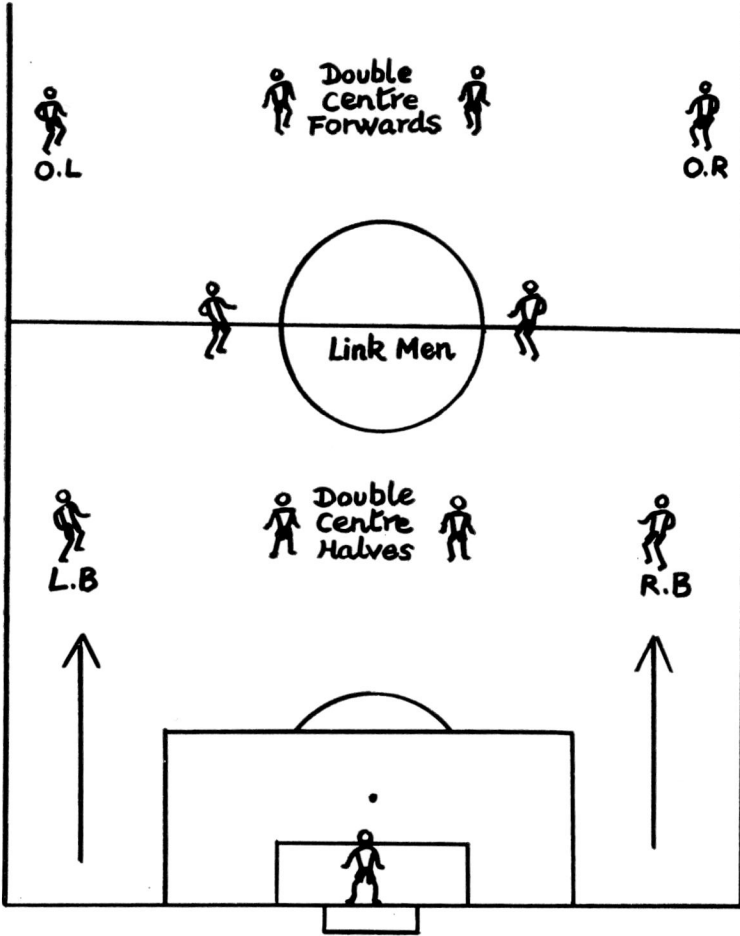

FIG. 22. The 4-2-4 formation

inside-forward and a wing-half) and four thrusting forwards. It
is a particularly good method of countering a double centre-
forward menace from your opponents, and, if working properly,
it should give you six players on attack and six on defence when
needed. But, this system throws an enormous amount of work

75

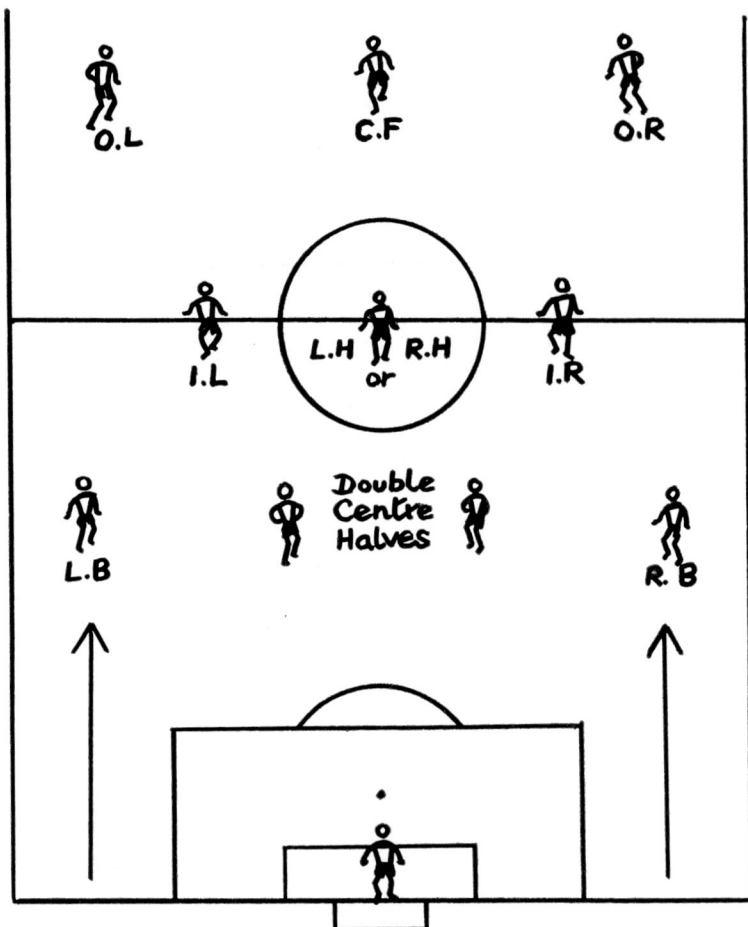

FIG. 23. The 4-3-3 formation

upon the two 'link' men, and unless they possess great stamina and outstanding ball control, the 4–2–4 formation can backfire very sadly.

3. *The 4–3–3 formation*

The 4–3–3 system sprung into prominence with England's

victory in the 1966 World Cup, and immediately many teams adopted Sir Alf Ramsey's formation without realizing the advantages and disadvantages of the system. Defensively the rearguard of four is exactly similar to the defensive line of 4–2–4; but, as you can see, in 4–3–3 another thrusting forward is pulled back to give your team three players linking in mid-field (see Figure 23). This means that seven players (the rear four and the midfield three) are available for defence, and six (the front three and midfield three) for attack if necessary. But, again, it is all too easy to allow this to become a strong defensive system, while the attack is outnumbered.

In 4–3–3 (and many of the variations on this) it is essential for one or more of the midfield three, or one of the full-backs, to strike from behind in order to penetrate a close marking defence, and this is why we hear so much about overlapping (see Chapter 3) and why we nowadays find so many defenders making and scoring goals in their opponent's penalty area. But remember that in a well-organized team no defender moves up into attack unless a colleague drops back to cover him.

Another very common position in football today is that of *sweeper*. The 'sweeper' is simply a deep-lying defender who 'sweeps up' behind his defensive line, not marking any particular opponent, but covering his full-backs or his central defence. A sweeper can be employed in a 4–2–4 or 4–3–3 formation (e.g. a centre-half covering behind the deep wing-half)—but he is increasingly used in an even more defensive system (shown in Figure 24) sweeping up behind a line of four other defenders, usually known as the Catenaccio system. Thus we find many modern teams—especially when playing away from home—adopting a heavily defensive formation of 1–4–3–2, which sometimes becomes one (sweeper)—eight (defenders)—one (attacker)! What a bore for the spectators!

You can't blame professional clubs (whose livelihood the

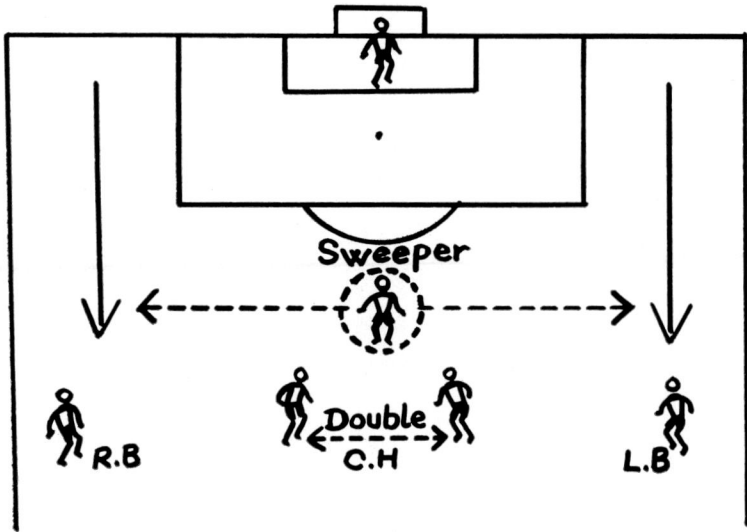

FIG. 24. The 'sweeper'

game is) for becoming so defensively cautious; but, whatever formation your team adopts, remember that football is at its best when it is played as an attacking game—as the Hungarians of 1954, the Brazilians of 1958 and 1970, and the Portuguese of 1966 have so wonderfully reminded us.

5

Learning from the Professionals

We all love to support 'our team' whether it be 'The United', 'The Rovers', 'The City', our local amateur team or even our School Eleven, and on these occasions we become so involved in the performance of our team, so worked up about the result that we often fail to *learn* anything from what we have seen. No doubt all of you, either with your father or a friend, have at some time or another been to watch a professional game, and no doubt you enjoyed the atmosphere, the excitement and the goals. But did you really learn anything worthwhile about the game? Did you watch the football intelligently? Or, like so many spectators nowadays, did you merely shout fanatically for your team, and shout abuse at the opposition, the referee and the linesmen? Surely this is not the way to watch football! By all means enjoy yourself, get your money's worth, but make a point of learning from the experts. You will be surprised how much you can coach yourself and improve your football by intelligent watching.

You can either watch the general picture of play and appreciate a team's tactics, or, more profitably at your age, try watching a single player (preferably in your own position) for five to ten minutes *with or without the ball*. Bearing this in mind let us first look at:

The Goalkeeper

(*a*) Look at that goalkeeper and notice how he is never still—even when play is at the other end of the field; look at the position he takes up as the opposing winger is about to centre; and see how far he is prepared to advance from his goal-line to help his defence.

(*b*) Analyse the goalkeeper's use of the ball. Is he throwing it quickly and accurately? Why is he kicking it high and hard—is it because his tall centre-forward is waiting to head it on? Is he taking too long over those clearances? Why?

The Defence

(*a*) Notice how coolly and sensibly professional defenders often play their way out of trouble. Look at the way they so often *play the way they are facing*—even if it is briefly backwards! Count the number of wild clearances the full-backs make in a game. You will be surprised how few there are.

(*b*) Frequently you will appreciate that a defence is not tackling, nor even marking very closely in midfield. Notice how a half-back, if in doubt, will not rush into a tackle in midfield, but will back away 'containing' his opponent (do you remember the advice in Chapter 3). But look at that mass of defenders guarding the penalty area. You will note that there is no 'holding off' or loose marking here in the danger zone! Look at that fierce tackling, physical heading that is so vital near goal. If you watch closely you will observe that the best defenders are 'man watchers' *not* 'ball watchers'. This means that although they have one eye on the ball, they watch the forward they are marking like a lynx, when he is near the

37. *Positioning at a corner kick.* As the ball (above the corner flag) is on its way across, note the strong cover given by the full-backs on the goal line.

danger area. What positions do the defenders take up at a corner? How does it differ from your corner drill? Are the full-backs positioned on the goal-line as in photograph 37?

(c) Have you noticed, too, how often defenders pass the ball *to a forward's feet,* rather than in front of him? Take a closer look next time.

(d) Unfortunately there is usually such a noise at any professional match that you cannot *hear* the players, but they can hear each other and you might be amazed to realize just how much helpful talking does go on. If you watch carefully you can often see a forward warning his colleague of what is happening behind him. The shout of, 'Plenty of time, Jim,' is much more valuable than, 'Give us a pass, Jim.' Do you shout helpfully in your team?

The Attack

(a) One of the most instructive of all lessons to be learnt by watching a football match is that of *movement 'off' the ball*. Do you know the length of time an average player is in possession of the ball during a 90-minute game? Two minutes at the most! This means that for over 88 minutes we are playing football 'without the ball'! No wonder the best footballers in the world are those who play intelligently without the ball. Take a single player next time you watch and notice how he positions himself; where he runs; how he finds extra space for himself; when he sprints and how he rarely relaxes. How often for instance are you standing still on the left-wing while the ball is with your right-back? Watch the professional.

(b) Notice how professional footballers rarely run at one pace. Watch that sudden *change of pace* by a winger with the ball, or a centre-forward without it. Do you change pace often in a game?

(c) How often have you come away from a game you have watched blaming perhaps the centre-forward for having a bad game? But think back, wasn't it because the opposing centre-half marked him so well? Then there was that inside-forward who scored three goals—most impressive, but how well was he marked?

(d) On other occasions you will have joined in the applause for a winger's rocket shot, which strikes the post from a very narrow angle; but if you had been looking closely you would have noticed that he had only to pass the ball gently back, and the centre-forward was far better placed to shoot. You may also applaud a player who dribbles past five opponents; but did you notice the way in which he could have split the defence with a quicker pass to another of his forwards?

(e) Finally, you young forwards should note how often professional footballers are prepared to take a shot. Do you shoot enough?

General Tactics

When you watch a game of football there are several other general points to note:

(a) When the professionals warm up before the game, notice how they split into small groups, not all shooting at the goalkeeper, and how they stretch their muscles before the game starts. Do you give yourself time?

(b) Watch out for 4–2–4 or 4–3–3; the 'overlap'; the 'sweeper' and other methods mentioned in Chapter 4. Notice how many teams recoil back into a packed defence, and then suddenly spring out into counter-attack. Notice again how many teams claim most of the territorial advantage in a game and yet create fewer clear-cut scoring chances than the opposition. Why is this?

(c) What about the temperament of the players? Do you realize why some footballers play better in a crisis, whilst others become rattled and lose their tempers too easily? Self-discipline is of vital importance in football so take careful note!

(d) Finally listen to the crowd's comments. Are they knowledgeable? All too rarely, you will discover! How often do you criticize a referee or linesman, when you are 100 yards away (or even watching the game on television!); and he is on the spot—and fully qualified?

38. *The bicycle kick*. This beautifully balanced overhead kick shows just what the professionals can do with a football—and most gracefully, too. Here we see Marsh (Queen's Park Rangers) in action in the 1966 League Cup Final at Wembley.

Beware

Finally a word of warning. Let us remember that professional football, while teaching us so many good points, can also teach us many undesirable features of the game. Sadly some of the greatest club teams are most to blame in this respect. What sort of things am I referring to?

(*a*) Unpleasant and unnecessary fouling.

(*b*) Objecting to a referee's decision. Of course he sometimes makes a mistake (he is only human) but throwing the ball away or swearing loudly will not help—and the odds are that he knows far more about the rules than you do. (Try being a referee yourself!)

(*c*) Time wasting. When money is involved this is perhaps understandable (though never commendable), but certainly your game will prove more enjoyable for all concerned if you don't deliberately waste time.

(*d*) Appealing to the referee or linesman all the time. You will see the professional player doing far too much of this. Perhaps he is trying to put pressure on the officials, but don't bother to copy your hero in this respect. It doesn't help anybody in the end, all it does is lower your team's reputation for sportsmanship.

(*e*) Pretending to be badly hurt when you are not. Again this is not playing the game in the right spirit. Don't copy the professional player who puts on this sort of act.

(*f*) Hugging and kissing a goal scorer. There are always moments when one of our team scores a brilliant goal at a critical moment and instinctively we run to him and slap him on the back or shake his hand; such a reaction is only natural and no one can really object to this; but is there really any need to put on a display of exhibitionism whenever your team scores any goal? Does the mobbing and hugging of a footballer really help the image of soccer?

(g) Lastly you will see teams which play badly and are tactically unintelligent. Look out for this. Don't feel that the professional always knows more than you. In particular notice how many teams resort to the long chip into the penalty area from all angles—regardless of the strength of their forwards in the air—when it would be far more effective to keep the ball on the ground.

But when all is said and done few games can compete with the great combination of skill and stamina, imagination and discipline that soccer offers. Those of us who have played it, coached it and watched it have gained an enormous amount of enjoyment and made numerous lasting friendships. The more we know the game, the greater its reward. Whether you are a promising footballer or merely an enthusiastic one I hope that this short book will help you to enjoy more fully the greatest game on earth.

39. *Poise and balance.* Superbly demonstrated by Beckenbauer (W. Germany) as he calmly steers the ball past Mazurkieviez (Uruguay) to score his side's second goal in the 1966 World Cup quarter-final match.

6

Lessons from the 1970 World Cup

Since I wrote this book, the 1970 World Cup in Mexico has come and gone. What a wonderful fiesta of football it was, again attracting enormous interest throughout the world and keeping many of us glued to the television until the early hours of the morning.

No doubt you watched as many games as possible, read the newspapers avidly, and I am sure that you enjoyed the great moments of the competition—Pele's fabulous footwork, Mueller's goals, Bobby Moore's masterly performances, Italy's exciting semi-final against West Germany and the uninhibited exuberance of Rivelino and Jairzinho after they had scored. Great moments certainly, but what did you learn from the 1970 World Cup? How many fresh ideas, methods and tactics were on show in Mexico? In this short chapter I shall be looking more closely at the lessons to be learnt.

Perhaps the most exciting outcome of the 1970 World Cup was the amount of goals scored and the amount of attacking football played. Beforehand there had been many gloomy predictions of tough, defensive battles in Mexico—and certainly there were several such teams on view (Uruguay, Rumania and Italy, for example), but the quality of the attacking play provided by Brazil, West Germany, Peru, etc., happily outweighed dull and negative tactics. We can best understand the attacking successes of the Brazilians and the West Germans by looking more closely at their styles of play.

Brazil

You will remember that the Brazilians played a 4–2–4 formation and deservedly won the Jules Rimet Trophy outright, despite their rather suspect defence.

There are four features of their attacking play that I think you should remember:

1. *Their use of orthodox wingers*

It is true that both Rivelino and Jairzinho sometimes moved inside, or switched wings, but did you note the way in which they usually *stayed wide* and both had the ability to beat the full-backs *on the outside*?

2. *'Bending' the ball*

I have talked about this in Chapter 2 (see photograph 10), but in Mexico 1970 we saw the ball swerving and dipping more than ever before. The high altitude made a difference, but did you notice the South Americans kicking with the outside of the foot and *the inside of the foot* in order to swerve the ball round a defensive wall of 6 to 8 players?

Rivelino scored two outrageous goals in this way, but Gerson, Pele and Jairzinho hit some wonderful, cunning shots too. It is worth practising as soon as you find the chance.

3. *Unselfishness*

If you or I possessed as much skill as those Brazilian forwards, wouldn't we often try to dribble past defender after defender, and perhaps hold on to the ball too long?

Certainly there were some wonderful dribbles—do you remember Jairzinho's goal against Czechoslovakia, or Pele's amazing control against Peru? But it was the unselfishness of these great forwards, and their faith in each other that stood out.

Tostao typified this brilliant unselfishness. He was always prepared to take knocks, lay the ball into space for his colleagues and to lure marking defenders out of the danger zone. If you are a budding centre-forward, just study a film of Tostao and you will see a great player in action (off the ball and on). But Pele's perceptive passes to Jairzinho for the goal against England, and to Carlos Alberto for that final goal against Italy, were both examples of unselfishness quite apart from demonstrating so superbly the importance of pacing the pass.

4. *Imagination and Surprise*

Perhaps the biggest difference between the attacking play of the South American sides (especially Brazil and Peru) and the European teams (with the exception of West Germany) was their ability to do the *unexpected*. English and much European soccer has become increasingly systematized since 1966 and although these 'method' sides can cope with each other, there is no answer to imagination, flair and surprise. Do you recall that shot of Pele's from inside his own half that gave the Czechoslovakian goalkeeper a horrible shock? There were numerous examples of the unexpected pass—or shot—from Pele, Gerson, Tostao especially; and even if you do lack the remarkable individual skill of these players, remember that as a mid-field or a creative player, don't allow your imaginative play, or your surprise passes to be choked by an insistence on method. The two can be moulded quite happily by a good coach—as Zagallo the Brazilian manager showed!

89

West Germany

The other outstanding attacking side in Mexico was West Germany, not so talented individually as the Brazilians, but producing a brand of old-fashioned, attacking football that we can all learn from.

1. *Wingers*

Note once again how, like the Brazilians, the West Germans always played two wingers and by keeping Libuda and Grabowski (or Loehr) wide, gave more space in the middle for Mueller and Seeler to score the goals.

Once again it is worth recalling that the West Germans aimed at reaching the goal-line, followed by the centre or the pull-back, and no doubt you remember exactly how Grabowski went round Cooper (of England) to centre for the decisive goal in the quarter-final match. How often do you young wingers try to beat your full-back on the *outside* and reach the goal-line?

2. *The twin centre-forward*

Although Seeler did not always play up alongside Mueller as double strikers, these two West German attackers dovetailed perfectly. Do you remember how well they combined in the air, and how often Seeler headed the ball on to Mueller when he might have been tempted to head for goal himself?

If you really want to see heading for goal at its best ask your football coach to show you a slow motion film of Mueller heading against Peru, or of Pele's header against England.

3. *Fighting spirit*

While talking of Seeler and West Germany we shouldn't forget the importance in football—as in any team game—of team spirit, and the Germans (led by the indomitable Seeler) showed

40. *The decisive goal.* Mueller (W. Germany) scoring the third and decisive goal in the quarter-finals against England.

this vital quality in abundance in Mexico 1970. Perhaps you don't need reminding that the Germans were a goal (or more) down in every game they played in the Competition, that they pulled back from 0–2 down against the strong English side, and that they played the last match against Italy with their star player, Beckenbauer, severely restricted by a broken collar-bone. Whether we are talking of school, club or World Cup teams, that fighting spirit is an essential.

I have talked so far of the great attacking teams of the 1970 World Cup, but let us not forget that defence is just as important as attack in soccer tactics—(though not so exciting to watch)—and just as there were points to learn from a closer look at the Brazilian and West German attacking functions, so you de-

91

fenders should recall the tight defensive teams in Mexico—Italy, Uruguay, Rumania, U.S.S.R. and England. Despite the fact that the Italians did not concede a single goal until the quarter-finals, and also possessed two outstanding defenders in Rosato and Fachetti to bolster their Catenaccio system, the best defensive team in the 1970 World Cup must surely be England.

England

It has been said that England would have reached the Final of the World Cup (and even won it) if Gordon Banks had not been forced to miss that vital game with West Germany. Had this happened the success of Sir Alf Ramsey's team would have stemmed (as in the 1966 Final) from a defensive system. Let us look more closely at the outstanding features of that system and see what we can learn from it.

1. *4–4–2*
Playing 4–4–2 for most of the time, leaving only Hurst and Lee upfield, England usually had eight defenders when the opposition attacked, and this clearly strengthened the defence while limiting the attack. Bobby Charlton and Martin Peters were often criticized during the World Cup Series for not shooting more, but if you were watching closely you will have noticed that they were asked to operate largely in a defensive role in their own half.

2. *Cover*
In any good defensive system cover is essential, and the English defence was excellent in this respect. Do you remember the England *v.* Brazil match at Guadalajara? If those brilliant Brazilian ball-players beat one defender there was always another covering, and until Pele and Jairzinho found that one

space in the second half, the cover of Moore, Mullery, Labone, etc., was magnificent. Notice too, when Mullery, Cooper or

41. *Brazilian magic.* Jairzinho (*left*) fires the ball past England's goalie, Banks, to score the winning and only goal at Guadalajara.

Wright surged upfield how one of the forwards, Peters, Charlton or Ball, dropped back and covered for them. Do your forwards cover for your defenders in this way? Or are they two separate units?

3. *Confidence*

We have considered already the importance of faith in our colleagues on the football field, and this confidence that the English defenders show in each other is a large factor in their success. How often did you see the panic clearance from Moore and his men or the angry arguing between the defenders themselves? Not from Sir Alf Ramsey's team!

Of course, this confidence and assurance is enormously increased if a side contains two players as great and as calm as Bobby Moore and Gordon Banks, and, I think, in concluding

these impressions of the 1970 World Cup, it is worth looking
more closely at some of the qualities of these two stars.

4. *Gordon Banks*

You young goalkeepers should note especially Banks's lack of
fuss and unnecessary showmanship; his amazingly quick reflexes
(who can forget that remarkable save from Pele?); his courage
in diving at forwards' feet, and his wonderfully calm temperament which enables him to convey confidence to the rest of the
defence. You may not possess Banks's brilliant reflexes, but you
can spread confidence and calmness to your defence. Do you?

5. *Bobby Moore*

So much has been written about Bobby Moore that I won't
attempt to say it all again. But if you are a defender, there are
three aspects of Moore's play that you should try to emulate.

Firstly he *reads* the game so skilfully that he seems to have
more time than other defenders.

Secondly, he *times* the interception so well. For a man who is
not so fast, and not so tall as many of the forwards he is marking,
he judges his tackle and his jump to perfection. Notice how he
is often prepared to back away, to delay the advancing opponent, but, when he strikes, he tackles hard and invariably
comes out with the ball.

Thirdly, he *passes* with accuracy. Not for Bobby Moore the
constant (often negative) square pass; he is prepared to probe
the opposing defence with that amazingly accurate twenty to
thirty-yard pass straight to Lee's feet or Hurst's head—and
often played first time, too!

Study Bobby Moore's play next time you have the chance,
watch for these points and try to copy his timing, his long passing
and remember that the more you can read the game of football
the better player you will become.

94

Here, then, are just a few memories of the 1970 World Cup related to your understanding of the game of football.

Many teams and many fine individual players have had to be omitted in this short survey; but there is one aspect of the 1970 World Cup that we were all glad of (after the unpleasantness of 1966) and that was the good general level of refereeing and sportsmanship. Considering so much was at stake, the behaviour of almost all the great footballers in Mexico was excellent; and

42. *All that's best in football.* After the Brazil *v.* England game Moore (*left*) and Pele exchange shirts.

those of you who tend to curse your opponent after the game is over and walk off the field without a friendly word, just recall that magnificent moment after the Brazil *v.* England game when Moore and Pele exchanged shirts, smiles and handshakes. This, for me, exemplified all that was best in Mexico 1970.